Original title:
Chasing Cherries

Copyright © 2025 Creative Arts Management OÜ
All rights reserved.

Author: Jameson Hartfield
ISBN HARDBACK: 978-1-80586-264-2
ISBN PAPERBACK: 978-1-80586-736-4

The Taste of Togetherness

In a giggle of fruit, we take a ride,
With our hands in the air, let laughter collide.
Red cheeks and sweet juice, what a sight,
We stumble and tumble, oh what a night.

With baskets we race, a chaotic spree,
Slipping and sliding, oh can't you see?
The crow takes a peck, and we scold,
But who can stay mad at such treasures, so bold?

Sticky fingers and grins so wide,
We simply can't help but enjoy the ride.
Each berry we find sparks a new joke,
With each silly slip, pure laughter awoke.

So here's to the fun, let's savor the day,
With juiciness dripping in a humorous way.
Friends gather 'round, what a delightful mess,
In the orchard of giggles, we're all feeling blessed.

Ripe with Possibility

In the orchard, laughter flies,
Fruit so bright, it tempts the skies.
With a jump, I grab a snack,
Oh dear! That branch will not hold back.

Look at this, a berry showdown,
Who knew they'd make me wear a crown?
Juice drips down my eager chin,
Guess that's the way this game will spin.

Echoes of Euphoria

Underneath the sun's warm glow,
I leap and dive, what a show!
Got berries stuck both here and there,
A sticky mess, yet none to care.

My buddy swings with fruit-filled arms,
Saluting trees, their wobbly charms.
Chortles hide among the leaves,
Giggling stems in the softest reprieves.

Unveiling Hidden Treasures

In the bushes, treasures wait,
Squeezing through, oh what a fate!
Fruits elude my playful reach,
Pantomime of a fruiting speech.

Rummaging through grass so green,
I find a scale, so unforeseen.
With every dive, I slip and slide,
A fruity quest, a wild ride!

The Symphony of Juices

A symphony of color shines,
In every bite, a joyful sign.
Drumming hands on belly's round,
This berry party knows no bound!

With splashes bright, a feast unfolds,
Lyrics of laughter, truth be told.
Splat goes juice on the rabbit's hat,
Who knew that berries were so spats?

Crimson Pursuit

Ripe and round, the berries gleam,
I ran so fast, it felt like a dream.
Tripped on a root, fell on my back,
Wished I had wings for my little snack.

Laughter echoed through the trees,
As I dodged bees with childish ease.
The fruits above called out with glee,
'Come get us all, we're wild and free!'

Sweetness in the Breeze

A basket sways, it's filled with hope,
I climb a branch, looking to cope.
A squirrel steals berries, what a thief!
I shout, 'Hey buddy, that's my relief!'

The wind whispers secrets, oh so sweet,
As I dance around on my wobbly feet.
Is it the snack or the fun I seek?
Maybe it's both, I've hit my peak!

The Orchard's Whisper

Under leafy canopies, I prance,
Berry juice spills—a sticky romance.
Footsteps echo, they're not so sly,
Here come my friends, it's time to vie!

We giggle and race, striving to win,
Sharing stories mixed with some spin.
Who cares if we're covered in red?
It's the berry fun that fills our head!

Dancing Under Red Canopies

Underneath the red shade, we twirl,
Beneath our feet, the grass gives a whirl.
Berries plop in our eager hands,
Just like candy from fairylands.

With every bite, we burst into cheers,
Laughter erupts as we dodge our fears.
Nature's delight, in joyous spree,
In this fruity kingdom, we're wild and free!

Ripe Temptations on the Vine

In the orchard, a dance, so spry,
Bouncing under a bright blue sky.
Fruits hanging low, a jiggly tease,
Plucking away with the greatest of ease.

Laughter echoes, slips and trips,
Juicy love in every sip.
Sweetness drenching shirts and hands,
The best of plans lie in fruit stands.

Harvesting Daydreams

Baskets ready, the thrill is real,
With every hop, we spin and squeal.
Bright red globes, a cozy thrill,
With every reach, we tumble still.

Giggles burst with every snag,
The fruit brigade, a happy rag.
Who needs a map when you can roam?
Under the sun, we feel at home.

Secrets of the Scarlet Tree

Whispers of color, secrets unfold,
Beneath leafy hats, stories untold.
Swinging low, the branches sway,
As we giggle through the sweet buffet.

Mysteries hide in crimson hue,
Fruits that trick are ripe for you.
A mouthful of mischief, a world so bold,
Each bite a tale, each taste pure gold.

Frolic in the Fruitful Grove

In the grove, where shadows play,
We skip and hop the day away.
With every fruit, a giggle bursts,
Sweet surprises quench our thirsts.

Tickling branches as we climb,
Silly jumps, feeling sublime.
Soft laughter spills with every cheer,
As juicy treasures draw us near.

The Lure of Red

In a field where giggles grow,
I spied a fruit with rosy glow.
With a bounce, I tried to leap,
But landed in a pile—oh, deep!

Sticky fingers, faces smeared,
Friends in laughter, no one feared.
A berry thief in cotton socks,
Running wild among the flocks.

Tangled in Blossoms

Under branches, I did roam,
Lost in petals, far from home.
A little bee buzzed with glee,
Saying, "Stay here, and dance with me!"

I twirled around; I slipped and fell,
Into a bush, oh what a smell!
The blossoms sang a joyful tune,
As I wiggled beneath the moon.

Gathering Secrets

Whispers float on summer breeze,
As I gather fruit with ease.
Counting morsels, one, two, three,
Hmm, which one tastes most like glee?

Sneaking bites, in covert style,
Wearing a grin, oh such a wile!
My pockets bulge, I've lost my way,
But cherries laugh—"We'll make you stay!"

Beneath a Cherry Sky

Beneath the boughs, the shadows play,
Where laughter hides and kids run stray.
Trying to pluck the highest prize,
I nearly tumbled—oh, surprise!

With cherry juice, a painted face,
A sweet embrace, a sticky race.
We dance and prance beneath the sun,
In a world where antics are just fun.

Fragrant Footsteps

In the breeze, a scent so sweet,
Bouncing toes in dance and beat,
Laughter mixes with the thrill,
Chasing dreams on a hill.

Little hands reach high for treats,
Tiptoeing on all the beats,
A giggle here, a slip, a slide,
Joyful chaos far and wide.

With sticky fingers on the run,
All around, their faces spun,
We race the clouds, a funny chase,
In this sweet, berry-filled place.

A Treetop Odyssey

From the ground, we spy a prize,
Bright red gems against the skies,
With tiny hearts all set to soar,
We climb and climb for just one more.

Each slip and tumble brings a cheer,
The branches sway, we persevere,
A squirrel laughs, it joins our game,
While we forget our slight bit of shame.

Up we go, our mission clear,
With every giggle, there's no fear,
And though we topple, we shall find,
The joy of berries, sweet and kind.

Legacy of the Orchard

An orchard's whimsy shines so bright,
Where shadows dance in golden light,
With each hop, we claim our fame,
As sticky messes we proclaim.

Old trees watch as we make a scene,
Running wild, we feel like queens,
We swipe our prizes, giggling bold,
In their roots, our tales are told.

The sun dips low, day's playful end,
With cheeky grins, our hearts ascend,
For memories made beneath the trees,
Forever shared in the softest breeze.

Kisses from the Earth

Each berry picked, a little round,
An explosion of joy for us found,
A race to taste the sweetest face,
Journeying through the fruity space.

Barefoot breezes tickle our toes,
As laughter spills where sweetness grows,
With each bright bite, we bounce and roll,
Nature's candy fills the soul.

Muddy footprints mark our spree,
In this sweet hide-and-seek jubilee,
With every giggle under the sun,
We savor earth's kisses, oh what fun!

A Game of Sun and Shade

In the garden, shadows dance,
A sneaky game, oh what a chance.
Behind the bush, with giggles low,
I spot a red, that starts to glow.

We tiptoe near, with sticky hands,
A treasure hunt on sunny strands.
With every step, a laugh erupts,
As clumsy feet make tumbles and thumps.

The neighbor's dog gives us a stare,
With silly barks, he thinks it's fair.
We grab and run, our bounty caught,
With laughter louder than we thought.

As dusk descends, we share our score,
A mishap here, and so much more.
With stained faces and joyful cheer,
Tomorrow calls, we'll reappear.

Fragrant Adventures on Soft Grass

The field, alive with scents so sweet,
We bounce along, on little feet.
A picnic plan that's full of glee,
With wrinkled fingers, we count to three.

A sneaky squirrel gives us a glance,
While we plot our juicy little dance.
We weave through clovers, our laughter rings,
Imagining we're royalty, with silly kings.

The breeze tickles, oh what a tease,
As we plot ways to snatch with ease.
In this realm of tall, lush hues,
We'll fill our pouches with wild hues.

At twilight's call, we flaunt our haul,
In sweet delight, we share with all.
With every grin, a memory made,
Adventures bloom in sunlit shade.

The Color of Innocence

A splash of red on summer's face,
We giggle loud, in this wild place.
With hands outstretched, we leap and bound,
In innocence, our joy is found.

The grass tickles, our feet unshod,
As we play tag with the evening god.
Each little squabble a silly fight,
Over the treasure that shines so bright.

Our fingers stained, like little thieves,
We share our spoils beneath the leaves.
With every bite, a burst that sings,
In this moment, we are kings.

As night falls down, we lie in rest,
With twinkling stars, our hearts are blessed.
In the tales we weave, so sweet and pure,
This joyous game will always endure.

Wild Sweets in the Sunshine

The sun beams down, the day is right,
Our eyes are wide, hearts full of flight.
With grassy patches calling our name,
We rush ahead, this is the game.

A fleeting glimpse of color near,
We race each other, filled with cheer.
With every stumble on the soft ground,
We're pretty sure adventure's found.

Oh, the sticky snack that brings delight,
Is worth the chase in pure daylight.
While insects buzz and butterflies play,
We gather joy in the sun's ray.

As shadows grow and laughter fades,
We pack our treasures in leafy blades.
With cheerful hearts, we bid adieu,
Till next we meet, in our paradise anew.

Sunlit Wanderlust

In fields of red, we skip and hop,
A race for fruit, we shan't stop.
With baskets swinging, laughter rings,
As sticky fingers pull at strings.

The sun beats down, our heads a swirl,
With every bite, we giggle and twirl.
The nectar drips, oh what a mess,
Who knew a berry could cause such stress?

A squirrel steals one, we chase in vain,
Through bushes thick, it's all insane.
With every laugh, we lose the race,
But winning isn't our goal, just the taste!

So here we are, in joyful spree,
With shirts stained red, oh, can't you see?
Tomorrow's sun will shine anew,
But today is ours, with berries in view!

Serendipity in the Air

There's magic floating, sweet and rare,
With every breeze, I smell the fare.
The path is crooked, nothing planned,
But oh, how joyous is this land!

We step in puddles, splashes fly,
With every giggle, our spirits high.
The world spins 'round like a dizzy dream,
As berries taunt us with their gleam.

A dog barks loud, it thinks it's tough,
While we can't seem to get enough.
With laughter bursting, we make a mess,
Creating chaos, after all, it's best!

We lay on grass, a treat in hand,
No thought of rules, just berry demand.
Under the sun, our hearts take flight,
In silly bliss, we own the night!

Pilgrimage of the Palate

With every step, we seek the prize,
A juicy orb before our eyes.
We journey forth with lots of cheer,
Embracing flavors far and near.

The vines are tangled, branches scratch,
We jump and tumble for the catch.
A giggle here, a slip, a fall,
But in this quest, we've lost it all!

Red lips stained, we're berry-bound,
With trails of juice all around.
A race ensues, who can outrun?
The laughter echoes, oh what fun!

The day winds down, but joy won't fade,
In every berry, memories made.
With silly faces, we all unite,
Our palate's adventure, pure delight!

Nectar Under the Stars

Beneath the sky where wishes soar,
We plot our fun, we crave for more.
With starry dreams and lemonade,
Our midnight picnic's been well laid.

A flash of fireflies, sweet delight,
We pass the jar, our laughter bright.
The moon, a witness to our spree,
As we indulge, just you and me.

The crunch of leaves beneath our jam,
We're bursting forth like a wild slam!
With every bite, the world's our stage,
In fruit-filled fantasy, we engage.

The night's alive, we dance and sway,
Wrapped in joy, we laugh and play.
With full bellies and spirits high,
Under the stars, we'll never say bye!

The Art of Foraging

In a hat too big, I wander,
With a basket, oh what a blunder.
Beneath the boughs, I spy a treat,
My feet get tangled—what a feat!

The birds all laugh; they know my name,
As I trip and tumble, oh what a game.
A juicy glob slips from my grasp,
And rolls away with quite a gasp!

My friends all cheer from nearby trees,
"When will you learn? Just take it, please!"
But every pluck is a circus act,
And I must admit, it's quite a pact!

So here I stand, both proud and sore,
With tales of berries and forest lore.
Though I leave with more bruises than gold,
The laughter shared is worth more than told.

Beauty in the Boughs

The branches wave, with leaves that sway,
As I inspect each twinkling spray.
With sticky fingers and a grin so wide,
I reach for treasures that try to hide.

The squirrels conspire, they tease my quest,
As I climb up high, putting strength to the test.
I pluck and I plunder, my pockets are full,
But the branches are slick, oh boy, take care, fool!

Be careful! Look out! My friends all shout,
As I swing and swirl, caught up in my clout.
But I've got my sights set, no turning back,
Even if the bees have launched a sneak attack!

And at the end, with sun on my face,
I shuffle away with a new-found grace.
I may not be smooth, but that's alright,
For beauty in boughs always brings delight.

Sweets Beneath the Sky

Under the sun where shadows dance,
I plot and scheme for a sweet romance.
With a wink and a grin, I take my stand,
There's magic in the sticky hand!

A gust of wind sends leaves aflutter,
The laughter erupts—oh, what a clutter!
I slip, I slide, with flair and flair,
The prize eludes me, but that's fair!

Adventure calls—what a scrumptious game,
With berries bright, I stake my claim.
Friends roll their eyes, but join in the chase,
We're a merry bunch in this wild embrace!

So here we are, with spoils so sweet,
Singing out loud, our joy is complete.
Though we're messy and stuck like glue,
Who knew that berries could bring such a crew?

A Palette of Possibility

Brushes of laughter and splashes of fun,
With each little berry, the day's begun.
I gather my crew, we paint our fate,
And plunge into quests, never too late!

Colors of summer, a rainbow of fruit,
The trees stand tall, oh, what a hoot!
We mix and match with giggles and glee,
Inspiring joy like a berry spree.

Each pluck's a stroke, a masterpiece bright,
With every tasting, we soar to new height.
Splattered with juice, we're quite the sight,
An artful affair from morning till night!

So gather your friends, let's make some noise,
In the world of fruit, we are the joys.
For every mishap is part of the ride,
In this crazy world, let laughter be our guide!

Stolen Sunlight

I climbed a tree, oh what a sight,
To catch a glimpse of red delight.
A squirrel laughed, he knew the game,
As I reached out, feeling quite the same.

The sun peeked out from clouds of gray,
While berries danced in sunlit play.
I tried to grab them, oh so sly,
But missed the catch and fell nearby.

With branches cracking, leaves of green,
I vowed next time I'd chase the seen.
Yet laughter echoed through the glade,
As I tumbled down, my plans betrayed.

But joy is found in silly falls,
With berry stains, the laughter calls.
A lesson learned, in nature's fun,
Next time I'll just bring a running gun!

In the Shade of Boughs

Underneath the leafy dome,
I found the fruit, a sweetened home.
Yet every snagged, delicious bite,
Was guarded well by bees in flight.

I swatted left and ambled right,
As buzzing friends decided fright.
A honeyed truce was quite the feat,
To trade a dream for berry treat.

The laughter rose like summer's heat,
While dodging wings – I hit my seat.
With juice-stained fingers, mischief made,
I claimed my prize, despite charade.

And in that warmth, the fun was grand,
Creating chaos, quick and planned.
So here I sit, with tales to share,
Of berry jumps and buzzing air.

Whispers of the Grove

In grove so deep, where shadows play,
I heard the fruits call out, 'Hooray!'
Soft winds would whisper, 'Come and feast!'
But little did I know the beast.

A raccoon strutted, full of glee,
With berry stains just like on me.
We locked our eyes in berry war,
And giggles echoed from the core.

With sneaky paws, he made his claim,
As laughter flew, igniting the flame.
I chased him past the bending trees,
Beneath the hum of buzzing bees.

In this dance of wit and haste,
Hilarity became a taste.
The wild grove would echo back,
Our berry feud, a joyful snack.

Harvesting Dreams

With basket small, I came to seek,
A harvest bright, but oh so meek.
Each cherry plucked, sent joy in flight,
As sunbeams laughed, embraced the light.

But every step would set me off,
As roots and twigs would steal a scoff.
Down to the ground, I'd tumble free,
To chase my dreams, yet miss the spree.

A grandma's wink, she found much fun,
As I rolled by, avoiding sun.
She offered me a bowl of fare,
A treat to share, with no despair.

So here I sit with berry pie,
With humor shared, beneath the sky.
Harvesting laughter, dreams so bright,
In every bite, a sweet delight.

Echoes of Berry Bliss

In the orchard, I prance with glee,
A bucket's my hat, oh joy, can't you see?
The fruit on the trees just giggles and sways,
I dance like a fool, lost in berry-filled days.

With every step, I bump into bees,
They buzz in a choir, 'We want what you tease!'
I'm leaping and laughing, such silliness wide,
As I tiptoe through vines like a fruit-laden tide.

A drop of juice splatters onto my nose,
Each berry explosion a comic grand show.
I slip on the grass, and oh what a sight,
Rolling like laughter beneath the bright light!

But as I reach up for one juicy prize,
A squirrel grabs it first—oh, surprise, oh surprise!
With a wink and a twitch, he scampers away,
Leaving me chuckling at the end of my day.

The Chase Through Golden Light

Golden sunbeams dance on the ground,
I dash through the leaves, oh what joy to be found!
Red globes taunt me high in their throng,
My antics are silly—the chase is too strong!

I leap like a rabbit, quick as a wink,
But the branches are tricky, they giggle and clink.
The wind plays a game, it swirls in my hair,
With every close catch, I tumble and flare.

Look at that berry, so juicy and ripe,
Just out of my grasp—oh, they know how to hype!
In a dance of clumsiness, I spin and I dash,
As giggles erupt with every near crash.

But just when I thought I might capture a sweet,
A crow swoops down and takes it—ain't that neat?
Flailing my arms, I laugh at the mess,
Chasing these dreams, oh what a jest!

Beneath Pinks and Greens

Beneath the pink blooms and green leafy shade,
I frolic like a child, my worries just fade.
The fruit is a tease, hanging bright on the vine,
I leap for a handful, but land on a pine!

With laughter and giggles, I tumble and roll,
The earth and the berries—they're taking a toll!
A bush full of joy, so ripe and so round,
"Catch me if you can!" the sweet fruit calls out loud.

I stumble and bumble, a riotous spree,
Picturing pies, with a chuckle and glee.
But the tougher the chase, the more fun it seems,
In the heart of this orchard, I dance out my dreams!

Beneath the blue sky, I spin like a top,
Until one cheeky berry says, "Don't ever stop!"
With bites of the wild, there's nothing but cheer,
In the garden of giggles, sweet summer is near.

A Red Streak Across the Sky

Running fast, I'm a comet on the run,
In a fruit-fed frenzy, oh look at the fun!
The clouds chuckle softly, they tease 'catch me if you will,'
But the berry brigade answers, 'Let's see you stand still!'

I bound through the garden, a circus gone wild,
Every tumble and fall brings out my inner child.
A splash of red juice drips down my chin,
With a wink of mischief, I take it on the spin!

Every berry around me just giggles in bliss,
A roguish adventure—oh, what did I miss?
As I reach for a horde, a bird swoops on by,
To steal my sweet treasure—a red streak in the sky!

But laughter erupts like fireworks at night,
Because even the berry knows it's a funny sight.
With twirls and with spins, I'm the star of the game,
In the orchard of giggles, nothing's ever the same!

The Color of Desire

Crimson globes on leafy boughs,
A gentle tug brings laughter loud.
I climbed too high, oh what a show,
As gravity pulls, down I go.

My basket waits, a clever thief,
With sticky hands, I grin in grief.
Each berry plucked, a joyful sin,
Is this the sweetness where we begin?

A tumble here, a stumble there,
My friends just laugh, they do not care.
The leaves conspire, the branches sway,
In this ripe game, we'll laugh and play.

So here's to fruit that loves to tease,
A burst of joy with every squeeze.
The color bright, it draws us near,
With each sweet taste, we shed our fear.

Ripeness on the Wind

Breezes play with fruits so round,
They dance like clowns upon the ground.
A cherry drops, a clever trick,
Oh look, a red kite up so quick.

We race through fields, hearts in a whirl,
As nature laughs, our banners unfurl.
The juicy drops call out to me,
Yet still I trip on roots of glee.

An orchard wonder, oh such a sight,
With birds that sing and kids in flight.
The whispers float, a fruity tune,
As laughter echoes under the moon.

Right in this moment, we let it flow,
The ripeness sings, we steal the show.
With every giggle, the world feels bright,
In this buffet of summer's delight.

Dappled Hues and Hopes

Under the shade, we seek our prize,
Pockets filled with treasure and lies.
A splash of red, a wink of green,
Each fruit we find is fit for a queen.

The leaves above start to chatter,
It's not just fruit, it's all that matters.
A tumble here, a bruise so sweet,
The ground catches me, a mischievous seat.

We map our quest by colored delight,
In laughter's glow, we'll take our bite.
With summer's blush, we claim our share,
No cherry left that's stripped bare.

Dappled hues bring us together,
With sticky hands in sunny weather.
Let memories bloom, fresh and alive,
In this fun chase, our spirits thrive.

Scent of Summer Days

In the orchard, scents do swirl,
Like candy dreams, they twirl and twirl.
A giddy chase through trees brings cheer,
But oh, that branch! I'll have to steer.

With laughter loud and giggles bright,
We scheme to reach that one last bite.
The sun above, a playful tease,
We scale the heights with laughs and wheezes.

A foot slips here, a hand slips there,
Flavors burst like wild affairs.
The joy we seek is far and wide,
Yet every stumble we just ride.

Scent of summer fills the air,
In fruit-filled frenzy, none could care.
With each bold bite and laughter's sway,
We harvest joy—what a fine day!

Where Laughter Drips

In the orchard, giggles bloom,
Red globes dangle, causing doom.
Fingers sticky, faces smeared,
A wild race, all laughter cheered.

Baskets tip, a friendly fight,
Fruit flies buzzing, what a sight!
Who will snag the biggest prize?
The fruit, it taunts, beneath the skies.

Smirks exchanged and laughter hurls,
As they tumble in sweet swirls.
Each bite's a joke, a juicy trick,
A gobble here, a cherry flick.

At sunset's glow, the games conclude,
With cheeks like moons, in merry mood.
A day well spent, no room for blips,
Just laughter dripping from our lips.

A Dance with Temptation

In the twilight, red orbs sway,
Tempting feet to dance and play.
Jumps and twirls, with fruit in hand,
A merry jig, the sweetest band.

Juicy beads fall with quick intent,
Foot stomps loud, as rhymes are bent.
Nature's tune, a cheeky beat,
With every bite, the laughter's sweet.

Spinning dreams, in sticky bliss,
A playful sass that none could miss.
Who knew fruit could bring such cheer?
A comedic waltz, the end is near.

As shadows blend and colors fade,
The dance persists, the fun won't trade.
With full bellies and hearts in trance,
Tomorrow calls for another chance.

Journey of the Juicy

On a quest for crimson delight,
A wild crew, in pure excitement flight.
Pits and laughs collide in cheer,
Each step forward, the berries near.

Our sticky hands, a treasure map,
In laughter's echo, we escape the trap.
Jokes are shared with every find,
The sweetest fruit, a playful bind.

With buckets full and hearts alight,
We stumble back in fading light.
But in our wake, a trail of fun,
Adventures shared, not just for one.

We toast the day with cherry juice,
In our mirth, there's no excuse.
Forever on this merry ride,
A journey sweet, with friends beside.

Elixir of the Earth

From trees above, the treasures drop,
With laughter high, we can't be stopped.
Juicy potion, nature's best,
A burst of fun, forget the rest.

Each plump bite, a hearty laugh,
We gather from the sunlit path.
Like little kids, our spirits soar,
As puddles form beneath the score.

The world's elixir, pure and bright,
With every cherry, we ignite.
Jests and quips, they fill the air,
In this sweet joy, we shed our cares.

As dusk arrives, we hold our spoils,
With sticky hands, and joyful foils.
A toast to laughter, life's own cheer,
In every bite, our joy is clear.

Tickled by Petal Rain

In the breeze, petals dance and twirl,
A little bird drops, it's quite a whirl.
Caught in a storm of pink and white,
I dodge and dive, what a silly sight!

Laughter rings through the leafy trees,
As bees buzz by, 'Oh, do you please!'
Petals land on my nose and cheek,
In this playful shower, I'm far from meek!

With every flutter, the world gets bright,
Nature's pranks are pure delight.
I skip like a child, feeling spry,
Under the skies, I'm flying high!

So, let them fall, these whimsical show,
In this petal rain, I'm ready to go!
With a heart so light, I'll roam and twirl,
Who knew a day could be so pearl!

Orchard Secrets: A Sylvan Quest

Hidden paths in the leafy maze,
I stumble upon a fruity craze.
Beneath the boughs, my treasure hunt,
What's that? A squirrel, on a stunt!

Eager to find the sweetest prize,
I peek behind the leafy ties.
The sun above, a cheeky guide,
Through the branches, I slip and glide.

A rustle, a giggle, what could it be?
A tiny fox with a gleeful decree!
Join the frolic, come sway and spin,
In this orchard, we all win!

Secrets whisper, the trees confide,
Life's a journey, let's enjoy the ride!
As laughter echoes in the sunlit glade,
These sylvan adventures never fade!

Juicy Revelations at Dusk

As twilight falls with a rosy glow,
I wander where the wild winds blow.
Berries glisten, a fragrant tease,
An invitation carried on the breeze.

With each bite, a burst of fun,
Sweet surprises before they're done.
A splash of juice on my chin, oh dear,
These evening snacks bring so much cheer!

The sun dips low, the stars take their post,
I toast to the flavors I love the most.
Laughter spills under dusky light,
What a delight, what a funny sight!

So here's to dusk and its juicy tales,
In nature's arms, joy never fails.
Every nibble, a giggle, a treat,
Adventures await with every sweet!

The Hidden Delights of Nature

Beneath the leaves, what good surprise?
Nature's treasure, oh how it flies!
With a hop and skip, I play the fool,
Swallowed whole by a cherry pool!

The laughter echoes, ricochets high,
As I duck and dodge with a playful sigh.
Sticky fingers and smeared-up cheeks,
Nature's charm, it forever speaks!

In the branches, little critters peek,
With mischief in heart, they share a cheek.
Jumping around in a silly spree,
Together we weave a joyful glee!

So here I stand, in nature's embrace,
Unveiling wonders with a cheerful face.
In the hidden delights, I'm never late,
Life's a party, let's celebrate!

Playful Pursuits

In the orchard where shadows play,
Little feet skip, oh what a day!
With sticky fingers and giggles loud,
We race with the wind, feeling so proud.

A ladder wobbles, a daring climb,
"Catch me if you can!"—a rhyme in time.
Fruit flies quickly, we sway and twirl,
Who needs a crown? We're kings of the swirl!

Under the trees, we plot and scheme,
To fill our buckets—oh, what a dream!
With laughter echoing, we hide from sight,
What a delicious, chaotic delight!

As twilight beckons, we munch and grin,
Even the squirrels join in our din.
Juicy smiles and dessert, oh please!
Who knew so much fun could come from these?

Enchantment Among Leaves

Carrying baskets, we tiptoe and sway,
Among bright branches, we hop and play.
With cherries bouncing, we squeal in glee,
Like amateur acrobats lost in a spree.

Giggles echo when one takes a dive,
"Next time, buddy!" we laugh and thrive.
Our playful spirits, oh, they soar,
In this joy-filled kingdom, who could want more?

The leaves whisper secrets, we lean in close,
Telling us tales of the heavenly dose.
But as they rustle, we tumble, we fall,
In this sweet, silly chase, we have it all!

With cheeks rosy red and crumbs in our hair,
We dance like wild things, unaware of a care.
Moonlight peeks shyly as day bids adieu,
Leaving behind magic, just for us two.

Rendezvous with Radiance

Under a sunbeam, we plot and plan,
For a rendezvous only we understand.
With each stolen wink and mischievous grin,
A mission of joy where mischief begins.

We dart through the bushes, we zigzag and zoom,
Creating a whirlwind, all in full bloom.
In this tomfoolery, we gather with cheer,
Each plump, juicy treasure, our prize drawing near.

The trees sway gently, they join in our dance,
While fruit falls like confetti—what a chance!
Our laughter erupts, it's a melodic spree,
We toast with our treasures, just you and me!

As dusk draws its curtain, we twirl hand in hand,
With a handful of magic, we take our stand.
Under twinkling stars, our spirits roam free,
In this playful rendezvous, just you and me.

Whimsy in the Wilderness

In the wild, we wander, so carefree and bold,
With pockets of dreams and stories untold.
"Quick! Let's race!" oh, who will win?
With laughter like music, our whirls begin!

A silly squirrel chuckles, he knows the score,
As we leap through the leaves, begging for more.
With sticky red fingers and sun-kissed skin,
We crown ourselves royalty—let the fun begin!

Beneath a big bough, we plot and tease,
"Magic awaits if you just say please!"
The branch bends low, what's that lovely sight?
A glorious bounty, oh, what pure delight!

As the shadows dance, we laugh 'til we cry,
Playing hide and seek 'neath the sunny sky.
With giggles and whispers, we'll always recall,
This whimsical day, the greatest adventure of all!

Footprints on Soft Soil

In the orchard, mischief calls,
A race begins, we trip and fall.
Soft soil squishes between our toes,
With every laugh, the trouble grows.

A basket full of red delight,
We stumble onward, hearts so light.
Each step reveals a squishy surprise,
As muddy toes match grinning eyes.

Sticky hands, a bit of fun,
Smudges left from when we run.
Each cherry plucked, a sweet appeal,
Yet mud cakes on, a foolish deal.

Our shoes now wear a coat or two,
We giggle at the mess so true.
In our fingerprints, memories play,
On paths of mischief, we'll find our way.

Bouncing Between Branches

A leaping dance, we start to sway,
Between the boughs, we laugh and play.
An acorn drops, it's time to scoot,
We dodge, we weave, in autumn's loot.

Swinging high, oh what a sight,
A cherry hurls, we'll have a flight.
A tumble here, a twist and shout,
Caught in branches, there's no doubt!

With each bounce, our giggles grow,
A cherry crown upon my brow.
We pluck and toss, giggling bold,
While stories of our fun unfold.

Our laughter echoes through the trees,
As playful winds sing with the breeze.
In this wild, sweet fray today,
Sweet fruit above; oh, let's not stay!

The Glow of Harvest Light

Beneath the sun, our mission gleams,
A treasure hunt defined by dreams.
With goofy grins, we take our stance,
To fill our buckets in a dance.

The morning glow warms every face,
While sneaky squirrels start their chase.
We giggle wide at all their fuss,
As ripened fruit becomes the plus.

A slip, a slide, we grace the ground,
With laughter flourishing all around.
Each bounce brings joy, our spirits high,
As cherry snacks beneath the sky.

With every bite, our bodies squeal,
The sweetness of the moment feels.
In the light, as bliss ignites,
We dance and laugh till harvest nights!

Lifting the Lattice

Beneath the shade, we plot and scheme,
To reach the fruit of every dream.
With lattice lifted, we take a glance,
To seize our chance for one more dance.

A stretch, a jump, we climb and scour,
While buzzing bees take in the flower.
Through twisted vines and silly climbs,
We find the joy that feels like rhymes.

In cherry finds, our laughter spills,
We clink our baskets, all the thrills.
As pockets weigh with tart delight,
We cheer aloud, pure fun tonight!

With every berry safely stored,
We leave behind a world adored.
As shadows dance beneath the leaves,
We bask in fun that autumn weaves.

Grappling with Greenness

In a world so bright and red,
I tripped on roots, oh what dread!
The fruit above was ripe and sweet,
While I wrestled with my two left feet.

Leaves whispered secrets up so high,
I reached and lunged, with a goofy sigh.
The birds just laughed, perched in the tree,
As I rolled on grass, feeling quite free.

With arms outstretched like a crazy bird,
I swung and missed, oh how absurd!
The laughter echoed through the lane,
While I lay there, proud of my shame.

But finally, oh what a prize!
A single fruit, much to my surprise.
I bit right in, sweet juice did flow,
Tasting victory, or so I know.

The Race for Rapture

On a sunny day, with a grin so wide,
We raced to the orchard, hearts filled with pride.
Each friend was poised, with baskets in hand,
As we dashed through the grass, a wild, merry band.

But soon, oh dear, it was clear to see,
That my shoelace was tied to a nearby tree.
I stumbled and tumbled, rolled like a ball,
While my friends just giggled, as I made my fall.

With arms in the air, I struck a pose,
Claiming the title of Fruit-Picking Nose.
The fruits protested as they flew through the air,
Each catch a treasure, a moment to share.

At the finish line, with sticky green hands,
We counted our scores, and revised our plans.
With laughter and fruit stains all over the place,
We toasted our chaos, a remarkable race.

Beneath Petals and Promises

Under canopies draped in light,
We sought the treasures, a colorful sight.
But fell headfirst into a patch of mud,
With petals and giggles, we were a flood.

A promise once whispered, 'Let's pick the best!'
Yet I got tangled, my shirt was a mess.
The more I tugged, the more it would stick,
I laughed at my failure, what a funny trick!

The bees buzzed by, with mischief in mind,
They joined in the chaos, oh so entwined.
Captured in laughter, we danced all around,
As the fruits on the trees swayed to the sound.

And though we left with dirt on our knees,
We filled up our baskets, sweet as you please.
With jest and delight, we skipped down the lane,
Living for moments, making memories rain.

Echoes of the Picking

In a field where laughter is fruit's best friend,
We searched for the gems, just around the bend.
With each little hop, a wobbly gait,
The sweetness within kept drawing us straight.

But then came a squirrel, all boastful and brave,
He showed us his stash, as we watched him rave.
With soaring leaps and a cheeky grin,
We plotted our heist, let the fun begin!

I leaped like a champion, my aim was true,
But landed right next to a gentle moo.
With cows as my audience, I felt quite the fool,
As I stumbled again, breaking our rule.

Yet laughter rang out, as the fruits did collide,
We all shared the spoils, with joy and with pride.
In echoes of giggles, our hearts felt so free,
The best kind of picking, just you wait and see!

A Journey Through Blossoms and Stems.

In a garden lush and bright,
I danced and twirled with delight,
Leaves like hats upon my head,
Thinking of fruits that soon would spread.

With fingers sticky, I did climb,
A ladder built for cherry rhyme,
But slipped and landed on my rear,
The squirrels laughed, oh how they cheered!

Each tree a friend, each branch a tease,
I hollered loud, "Get down, you bees!"
They buzzed around, I waved with glee,
While gnawing on a branch for free.

Finally, I found my prize,
A bowl of red, oh what a size!
I celebrated, did a jig,
And accidentally dropped a fig!

Sweet Pursuit

With basket swinging by my side,
I raced the clouds, my joy my guide,
Each step a bounce on dewy grass,
A fruity war, I'd surely pass.

The sun wore shades, the breeze wore pants,
While I engaged in cherry dance,
A plump red rogue up on a limb,
Giggled down at my whimsy hymn.

"Just one more," I slyly mused,
As sticky fingers left me bruised,
The laughter of my friends nearby,
Made every reach a comic try.

My bounty spilled, like giggles in air,
Join in the fun, if you dare,
For in this chase, we lose all shame,
And end up sticky, laughing, aflame!

Orchard Reverie

In an orchard bright and fine,
I donned my hat, and sipped some wine,
With laughter echoing through the trees,
A banquet planned with fruit and cheese.

The rogue wind came, it stole my cap,
As I took aim and had a nap,
My mouth was wide, the cherries flew,
Like candy rain, and I, the goo.

A kite flew by—was it a bird?
I waved it off, my vision blurred,
In sweet delusion, I lost my way,
And ended up in quite a fray.

Trees crowded close, I bowed and spun,
In strewn fruits, I found my fun,
So here I sit, with glee bestowed,
In this orchard mad, my heart's abode!

The Fruitful Quest

On a quest for treasures bold,
With laughter bright, and stories told,
Each branch held secrets, sweet and rare,
But first, I must confront my hair.

With every stretch, a funny face,
As branches tugged my humor's grace,
A tumble down sent leaves to sway,
I rolled and laughed it all away.

The orchard's mirth was hard to bear,
With dogs and friends, we lit the air,
Each cherry claimed, a silly cheer,
And with each bite, we'd shed a tear.

Fruits aplenty, sunshine bright,
Every moment feels so right,
In this funny game we play,
The sweet reward won every day!

The Sweetest Climb

Up the tree, I go with glee,
A wrinkled face, it's plain to see.
With every step, the branches sway,
I hope I won't fall, oh what a fray!

A goofy grin, I reach too high,
The fruit so near, oh me, oh my!
Slipping down with all my might,
My friends below are in for quite a sight!

Sticky fingers, laughter loud,
As I tumble, part of the crowd.
Climbing back, I'm on a quest,
For juicy wonders, oh, it's the best!

But here I stay, caught in jest,
Hanging low, no time to rest.
Those cherries bold, they tease, they jive,
I'll get them soon, I'm still alive!

Lifting Hearts and Branches

A step inside this berry spree,
With sticky hands, I grin with glee.
Swinging high, I'm lost in thought,
While ducking low, I dodge the caught!

My pals are here, with nets galore,
They lift me high, I beg for more!
The trees above, they shake and sway,
As we concoct our fruity play!

A cherry pit flies through the air,
I duck and twist, I'm light as air!
With laughter bursting, we perform,
In this wild, tasty, candy storm!

Leave reason behind, this fun's so bright,
The fruit's allure is pure delight.
Here we'll dance 'till daylight's wake,
For hearts and branches, one big shake!

An Invitation to Indulgence

Gather 'round, come join my spree,
A fruity treat awaits with glee!
The trees are ripe, the sun is high,
Come on, my friends, let's reach the sky!

Wobble on limbs, as giggles burst,
A fruity mission, we'll quench our thirst.
Outfit stained with cherry red,
We'll jump and wiggle, nothing to dread!

A basket big, it's surely cursed,
Each leap and laugh, the thrill's rehearsed.
Who's in the lead? It's hard to say,
The sweetest prize is always just a sway!

So grab a branch, and hold on tight,
Let's swing through dreams, with pure delight.
An invitation, come share the fun,
With every bite, we're never done!

Searching for Bliss

Through leaves and laughter, I embark,
With every step, I make my mark.
The mission clear, I spin and twirl,
For juicy treasures, in a whirl!

A plump delight, just out of reach,
I dance around, I start to screech!
With antics wild, I'm in a chase,
A funny fumble, a fruity race!

The sun is bright, the bugs are bold,
An epic tale of fruit unfolds.
I trip and flip, with arms spread wide,
Just one more reach, I take a ride!

But what's this? My foot's a mess,
I tumble down, but don't confess.
A cherry smiles as I land with grace,
In this adventure, I've found my place!

Aroma of Nostalgia

The scent of spring fills the air,
Memories dance without a care.
Running fast with laughter bright,
Catching dreams in pure delight.

Baskets flop, and laughter flies,
As fruit above us blocks the skies.
With sticky hands and silly grins,
We gather joy in playful spins.

A splash of juice on eager cheeks,
Ticklish moments, laughter speaks.
Once upon a time with glee,
We were ripe and wild and free.

In every bite, a tale unfolds,
Of friendships sweet, and tales retold.
Oh, the joy of every pluck,
In childhood's orchard, we found luck.

The Pursuit of Juiciness

A sprint, a leap, a playful chase,
Round the tree, I set my pace.
With grass stains and shrieks of mirth,
My heart's aglow, it knows its worth.

The sun shines bright, a juicy prize,
With every bite, a new surprise.
Slippery hands and sticky feet,
In this hilarious, fruity feat.

Friends unite in berry fights,
We're drenched in sweetness, what delights!
A race to munch, a race to snack,
Each giggle echoes, never lack.

Though tangy drops may land on clothes,
Our giggles sprout like blooming rose.
With every lick, our voices sing,
The juicy joy that summertime brings.

In the Company of Blossoms

Amidst the blooms, we romp and play,
Each petal tickles in a sway.
Up and down, we twist and dive,
In nature's lap, we feel alive.

A bee buzzes by, oh what a tease,
As I swat at it, I feel the breeze.
With friends beside, we skip and hop,
Our hearts a-thump, they'll never stop.

Blossoms sway, like laughter shared,
With faces smeared, we're unprepared.
What's that on your nose, oh dear?
A flower crown, let's spread some cheer!

In this daft garden of delight,
We twirl and spin from morn till night.
Hand in hand, we trip and fall,
In the company of blooms, we have it all.

Tender Fruits of Fancy

In orchards bright, our spirits soar,
With tender fruits we can't ignore.
Plump and round, they call my name,
In this grand game, I'm not to blame!

With each pluck, a comic slip,
Down I tumble, what a trip!
Laughter echoes through the trees,
As I bounce back, I feel the breeze.

We trade our finds, an equal share,
All sticky sweet, without a care.
A fruit fight starts, we dodge and weave,
In playful mirth, we do believe.

The taste of summer, joy is spun,
With every bite, I feel the fun.
Tender moments, so bright and wide,
In this fruity dream, we take a ride.

Adventures in Abundance

In a field of fruity delight,
I tumbled and rolled in sheer glee,
With a basket that seemed way too tight,
I laughed as they danced from the tree.

Sticky fingers, a berry explosion,
I slipped and I wobbled with flair,
My friends joined in the sweet commotion,
As juice dripped down without a care.

We spun in circles, a merry ballet,
Competing for bites of pure bliss,
While birds chirped a cheeky ballet,
Little did we know what we'd miss!

At the end of the sun-drenched spree,
We nibbled on fruit covered in goo,
With laughter still ringing, we agreed,
Next time, let's wear a big bib or two!

A Song of Berries

A melody sweet as a fruit stand,
We sang with our hearts full of cheer,
Plucking gems from the green land,
Each bite melting away all our fear.

Tiny treasures in the tall grass,
Squealing with joy at each rosy find,
As sticky as honey, oh what a blast,
We giggled and danced, feeling unlined.

A tune played by our laughter,
Accidental splashes of berry juice,
Our song echoed, climbing ever after,
A symphony sweet, with less excuse.

So here's to the days of berry bliss,
Where silliness spun frames of delight,
Those fruity moments, we surely miss,
The songs we sang, oh what a sight!

Nature's Embrace

In the orchard where laughter is born,
We pranced like wild critters in spring,
Amid leafy green, we felt the morn,
And danced under the sun's bright wing.

Each tree held secrets, sweet and sublime,
We hid and we sought without a clue,
Chasing shadows, making up rhyme,
A spectacle of mischief that grew.

The earth tickled toes, where we spun,
As birds overhead sang silly songs,
The thrill of the chase, oh so much fun,
In nature's arms, where we belong.

So let's embrace this joyful spree,
With laughter echoing high and loud,
In the wild embrace, we'll always be,
Like joyful children, lost in a crowd!

Cartwheels in the Orchard

Round and round, we spun like tops,
Cartwheels made me feel so free,
While berries marched, the fun never stops,
My friends cheered loud, just wait and see!

Laughter erupted like a fizzy drink,
As I flipped and flopped in the grass,
With every whirl, we began to wink,
Caught in this moment, let joy amass.

The trees were our audience, swaying high,
As nature clapped with leaves all around,
In this bouncy, merry, silly sky,
We twirled together, joy unbound.

So let's cartwheel and giggle some more,
With juice dribbling down every chin,
Let's create memories we all adore,
In this cheerful orchard, let's twirl and spin!

Savoring the Journey

In a field of red delights,
A plump fruit takes to flight.
With every leap and bound we make,
We race to grab that juicy cake.

But oh, the trees are quite tall,
My friend trips and starts to sprawl.
Laughter echoes through the air,
As berries fall from everywhere.

The fruit fights back, it's quite a thrill,
It rolls and bounces, can't stay still.
We dive and tumble, what a sight,
A berry battle, pure delight.

In the end, we sit and munch,
With sticky hands, we share our lunch.
For every mishap, giggles bright,
Make sour days a sweet delight.

Under the Canopy of Delight

Beneath a sky so wide and blue,
We spot a tree with fruits anew.
With a whoop and a joyful cheer,
We scamper forth to gather near.

Each pick brings grins, and strange contort,
As one friend tries an acrobat's sport.
A berry hits the ground with a splat,
Then everyone laughs – how about that!

We dance around and chase the breeze,
With leaves that tickle, oh such tease.
Ambition high, our bellies ache,
For every pluck, a silly mistake.

We feast on fruits, both sweet and round,
With laughter, our joy knows no bounds.
In every pit, a story spins,
While nature's bounty brings us grins.

Whispered Wishes of Woodlands

In moonlit woods, we skip and sway,
The juicy gems lead us astray.
A mischievous sprite gives us a wink,
Handfuls of fruit make us think.

One climbs high, with hopes to reach,
A branch too far – oh, what a breach!
He tumbles down with a fruity smack,
And bursts of laughter ignite our track.

We gather gems, red as our cheeks,
With every slip, another laugh peaks.
The forest cackles, it knows our game,
No shame in the fun, it's never the same.

With each small bite, stories unfold,
Of roguish chases in shades of gold.
In wild abandon, we find our joy,
In cheeky mischief, kid and coy.

To Touch the Divine

A picnic spread on grassy ground,
Our mission clear – sweet treasures abound.
As we peek up, the branches sway,
Fruit dreams dancing, come out to play.

But oh, the struggle, a comical scene,
As one friend falls in a puddle, so green.
Mirth erupts, no dignity saved,
With berry juice, our fate engraved.

With every taste, we raise our cheer,
How many bites till we disappear?
Tummies full and laughter loud,
We wear our joy like a proud shroud.

As the sun fades, our smiles stay bright,
From silly antics, pure delight.
In juicy bites or a fall from grace,
Life's little joys, we warmly embrace.

Laughter Beneath Blossoms

In a garden of pink, we dance with glee,
Fruits hang low, just waiting, you see.
With each pluck, we giggle, oh what a sight,
The juice drips down, oh what a delight!

Silly faces made, sticky hands too,
Whispers of mischief, just me and you.
Beneath swaying branches, we leap and bound,
In this fruity frenzy, joy can be found!

We spot a bee and let out a scream,
Then share a laugh, it feels like a dream.
Pies and puddings, oh what a treat,
All the best moments taste oh so sweet!

So here in the shade, let's take a break,
With giggles that echo, make no mistake.
Nature's a playground, come join the fun,
With laughter and fruit, we bask in the sun!

Stolen Moments in July

Under the sun, we sneak a few bites,
Caught in the act, amidst summer delights.
With fingers all sticky and grins ear to ear,
Every little nibble brings us good cheer.

Caught in a tangle of laughter and glee,
The neighbors are watching; oh, do we agree?
With faces like clowns, we bumble about,
It's pure bliss—no hint of a doubt!

A challenge arises: who can eat more?
With cheeks full of fruit, we fall to the floor.
Outrageous our antics, with giggles we cheer,
A summer tradition that's oh so dear!

As daylight fades, we gather our loot,
Crammed full of berries, we're ready to scoot.
Stolen moments shared, no need to deny,
In this berry madness, we're flying high!

A Tapestry of Juicy Dreams

In a world filled with hues of cherry red,
We weave our tales with laughter ahead.
Crafty schemes over bowls piled high,
A juicy affair that makes spirits fly.

Each bite a burst of sweetened laughter,
In this whimsical land, who's the master?
A juggling act of fruits in the air,
Off our balance, we tumble with flair!

Friends all around, with stories to share,
Covered in juice, we dance without care.
Cakes in the oven, aromas divine,
Friendships are rich, like the ripest wine!

So let's daub our faces, a sweetened spree,
With each goofy grin, let the world see.
In this tapestry spun of silly delight,
Every moment we share feels simply right!

The Dance of Summer Fruits

With a spin and a twirl, the summer unfolds,
Fruits in a frenzy, their stories retold.
Juicy confetti rain down all around,
In our fruity fiesta, joy is the sound.

Step aside and watch; we're here for a show,
Mischievous moments that ebb and flow.
As laughter erupts, we stumble and sway,
These juicy treasures yell, "Come out and play!"

We wear matching hats, each one more bright,
Juicy laughter echoes deep into night.
The more that we share, the sweeter the tune,
Summer's a party beneath the full moon!

So come join the fun, let's dance and delight,
In a carnival spirit that feels so right.
With sweet treats in hand, we leap with a cheer,
In the dance of the season, our joy is clear!

Gifts of the Sun

A round red globe up in the air,
It winks at me with fruity flair.
I stretch and reach, but oh, so vain,
The tree just giggles, what a pain!

With baskets near, I plot and scheme,
To snatch the prize, oh what a dream!
But squirrels stare as if to say,
'You'd better hurry, it's now or nay!'

A clumsy slip, I hit the ground,
The cherries laugh without a sound.
I dust my pants and try again,
That tree's got jokes, oh what a friend!

At last, a branch I finally climb,
But all my efforts seem to mime.
They tease with color, bright and bold,
'Thanks for the dance, now watch me roll!'

Dreams on a Branch

Suspended high, the fruit does sway,
I try to snatch it, hip hooray!
But every time I grab in haste,
It's like a game of fruity waste.

Around I twirl, a merry spin,
The cherries giggle, where to begin?
They cheer me on, a fruity crowd,
While I perform, so brave, so loud!

I ponder dreams of jams and pies,
While squirrels roll their beady eyes.
'You'll never catch us up so high,'
They chant in chorus as they fly!

With one grand leap, I make my mark,
A big mess made, oh what a lark!
They scatter down, a juicy rain,
I've made a splash, but who's to blame?

The Allure of Lushness

Oh, how they shimmer, gleam, and shine,
Each little orb, a sweet design.
I waddle close and lick my lips,
As visions dance of cherry dips.

Why do they dangle, just out of reach?
Teasing my heart, oh how they preach!
With every bounce, my hopes ascend,
But then the wind gives me a bend.

At times they sway, like life's grand tease,
I laugh aloud, drop to my knees.
Just one good jump, I swear I'll win,
But up I go, then down again!

Each summer day, a jester's game,
These luscious fruits, oh what a claim!
I'll wear the crown of sticky hands,
And dance upon my fruity plans!

Fables of Flavor

Once upon a time, in trees so spry,
Fruity tales would fill the sky.
They whispered secrets, sweet and sly,
Of jumbles, jigs, and pie oh my!

With every leap, I'd lose my shoe,
The cherries laughed, as if they knew.
I tumbled round, what a silly scene,
A fruity fool in fields of green!

I dreamt of feasts, with sprinkles too,
While branches giggled, who knew we flew?
They offered me a sundae bright,
As I clutched air, to take a bite!

So here's my tale of laughs and falls,
Of dancing fruits and echoing calls.
The fables blend, a wondrous cheer,
For all who seek the sweet, oh dear!

Beneath the Bough

Underneath the leafy shade,
A plump little fruit parade.
With giggles and sneaky grins,
We reach for the plump, juicy wins.

Socks covered in sticky red,
From a game best left unsaid.
Chasing the fruit and the fun,
We're bound to trip and then run.

Laughter echoes through the air,
As we pull each other's hair.
With juice dribbling down our chin,
Each bite feels like a win.

Under branches we all dance,
In nature's wild, silly prance.
Who knew that fruit could be such glee?
Oh, the joy of being free!

Sweetness in Flight

A fuzzy strut among the leaves,
With giggling friends and old beliefs.
Sweetness dripping from our hands,
We're rulers of this fruity land.

A jump and stretch, what's that up there?
A daring leap through the air!
To grab the snack of summer's treat,
Laughing as we land on our feet.

Playful chaos in the tree,
Sticky fingers, can't you see?
With every bite, a silly grin,
The battle of fruits about to begin!

So here we are, no time to stall,
With cherry dreams we've seen it all.
The sweeter things make us laugh high,
Oh my, oh my, we could touch the sky!

Silhouetted in Scarlet

Shadows dance beneath the sun,
As we plot our fruity fun.
Bright red gems hang from above,
Filled with laughter, joy, and love.

A crooked stick and a toss so high,
Watching them fall—we all sigh.
Dodging under branches' sway,
Our morning mischief on display.

Juicy victories fill the air,
With laughter rising without a care.
Stumbling, rumbling through the fun,
Who knew snagging fruit could be done?

A sticky mess, and what a plight,
But oh, our hearts are feeling light.
In shadow games and fruity plays,
Oh, the fun in summer's rays!

Following Breezy Serenades

In the breeze we chase the sound,
Berry whispers swirl around.
With every gust, our hearts take flight,
Silly giggles fill the night.

Following tunes, a dance of cheer,
As fruity odors draw us near.
We twirl and tumble, joy abound,
In this lyrical playground.

Grass stains patch our eager knees,
With each brave leap, we feel the breeze.
The symphony of reds and greens,
In our messy, sweet routines.

Swaying arms and voices bright,
Chasing dreams 'til the end of night.
Fueled by laughter, oh what fun,
We play and prance until we're done!

www.ingramcontent.com/pod-product-compliance
Lightning Source LLC
Chambersburg PA
CBHW060114230426
43661CB00003B/176